This book is a gift from

Text by Sophie Piper
Illustrations copyright © 2010 Dubravka Kolanovic
This edition copyright © 2016 Lion Hudson

Published by Lion Children's Books
an imprint of
Lion Hudson plc
Wilkinson House, Jordan Hill Road,
Oxford OX2 8DR, England
www.lionhudson.com/lionchildrens

ISBN 978 0 7459 6595 6

First edition 2016

Acknowledgments
"Jesus, friend of little children" hymn by Walter J. Mathams (1851–1931)

A catalogue record for this book is available from the British Library

Printed and bound in China, October 2015, LH06

My Bible
Story Book

Sophie Piper

Illustrated by Dubravka Kolanovic

LION
CHILDREN'S

Contents

In the Beginning 10

Noah and the Flood 16

Abraham and the Promise 22

Baby Moses 26

Daniel and the Lions 32

Baby Jesus   38

Jesus and His Disciples   42

Jesus and the Little Girl   46

Jesus and the Children   50

Hallelujah!   54

In the Beginning

Before there was anything, there was nothing.
   Nothing at all... except God.
   Then God spoke to the nothing: "Let there be light," said God.
   At once the light shone out: clear, bright, sparkling. "That's good," said God. "That's very good."
   Then God made the world and everything in it. And everything was very, very good.

Then God made the first people: Adam and Eve.

"I have made for you a paradise garden," God told them. "Please take care of it.

"It will give you everything you need.

"But beware of one tree. Do not eat its fruit. If you do, everything will go wrong."

All was well, until a wicked snake slithered by.

"God's being mean," the snake whispered to Eve. "God doesn't want you to eat the best fruit of all.

"Try some. You'll find out how good it is."

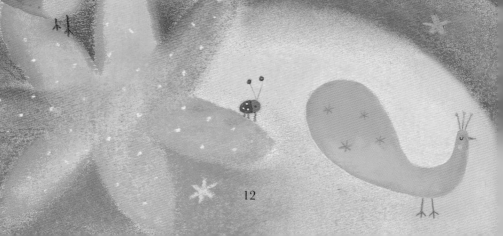

Eve picked a piece of fruit and bit it.
Mmm. It was good.
She gave some to Adam. "Mmmmm," he agreed.

From that moment, everything changed.

Adam and Eve knew they had done wrong.

God came and found them.

"Oh dear," sighed God. "You disobeyed, didn't you?

"You've spoiled the friendship with me and with the world. Now every day will just be work, work, work."

Adam and Eve were sad. Would they ever be friends with God again?

15

Noah and the Flood

Noah watched as the animals came by: two by two, by two – a mother and a father of every kind of animal.

"It's amazing!" said Noah's wife. "They're all walking onto your great big boat."

"It's all as God said it would be," said Noah. "God is sad about all the arguing and fighting in the world.

"God told me he is going to send a flood. He told me to build the boat – the ark – to keep us safe."

When Noah and his family and all the animals were on board, God shut the door of the ark.

Soon the rain came. The flood rose higher and higher.
The bad old world disappeared under the water.
As God had promised, the ark was safe.
Then one day, BUMP. The ark hit a mountaintop
that was hidden by water. It got stuck there because
the water wasn't very deep.

Noah let a dove fly out. It came back with an olive twig. The leaves were fresh and green.

"That's good news," said Noah. "There must be dry land somewhere. The flood is nearly over."

At last the land everywhere was dry.

"It's time to leave the ark," said Noah to the animals. "You must have families and start the world again."

As they set out, a beautiful multicoloured arch glittered across the sky.

"Look at the rainbow," said God to Noah. "It is the sign of my promise. I will never again flood the world like that. There will be summer and winter, seedtime and harvest for ever."

Abraham and the Promise

Abraham was a shepherd. His home was a tent. He would go wherever there was grass for his sheep and goats.

"One day," God told him, "This land of Canaan will be a home for your great-great-great-grandchildren. It will be theirs for always."

Abraham sighed. "My wife Sarah and I don't even have one child yet," he said.

"I am making you a promise," said God. "You and Sarah will have a son. One day your great-great-great-grandchildren will be as many as the stars in the sky."

But years came and went. Still Abraham and Sarah had no children.

One day some strangers came by.

Sarah listened as the men talked. "Next year," said one of the strangers, "we will come back, and your wife will show us your son."

Sarah laughed. "I'm too old to have babies now," she said.

"It will happen," said the stranger. "God has made a promise."

As the strangers left, Abraham and Sarah understood. They were angels, bringing a message from God.

By the next year, Abraham and Sarah had a son. They named him "Isaac".

The name means "laughter".

25

Baby Moses

When Isaac grew up, he married and had children.
His children had children. All was well in the land
of Canaan.

Then came hard times. For years there was no rain.
Abraham's grandchildren and great-grandchildren
moved to Egypt.

Years later, a wicked and cruel man became king.
"I don't want those incomers," he said.

"I shall make the grown-ups my slaves.

"I will tell my soldiers to find all the baby boys and throw them in the river."

One mother wove a basket and covered it with waterproofing tar. She put her baby son inside. Then she and her daughter Miriam went and floated the basket among the reeds of the river.

Miriam hid among the reeds to watch.
A princess came along to bathe in the river.

She and her servants saw the basket. They fetched it and peeked inside.

"A BABY!" squealed the princess. "I love him already."

Miriam came out from where she was hiding. "I know someone who will take care of that baby," she said.

She fetched her mother.

"I am going to make this baby mine," the princess said. "I have chosen the name 'Moses'. Please keep him safe for me."

Moses grew up as a prince in Egypt. He knew he was really one of the slave people. When he stood up for them, he got into trouble and had to run away.

In the wild country, God spoke to him.

"Go back to Egypt," said God, "and tell that wicked king to let my people go."

With God's help, Moses led the people back to Canaan.

On the way, he told them how to live as God's people should: loving God and one another.

At last the people made their home in the land that God had promised Abraham.

Daniel and the Lions

When the people lived as God's people should, all was well.

When they disobeyed, things went wrong.

One day, things went very wrong. A king from far away won a great battle. He took some of the people back to his land.

One of them was Daniel. "I shall do what is right even when everything is going wrong," he said to himself. "I shall always obey God."

Every day he worked hard in his job at the royal palace.

Every day he looked back to the land he called home, and said prayers to God.

33

34

Each new king had great respect for Daniel.

"I shall give him the best job," said the one named Darius, "because he's the best servant of all."

Other people in the palace were jealous.

They made a wicked plan. Then they went to King Darius.

"You need to make a new law," they said. "Everyone must trust you for everything.

"If anyone trusts anyone else at all, that person must be thrown to the lions."

"What a good idea," said the king. And he made the law.

Soon the men came back. "Daniel has broken your law!" they cried. "He puts his trust in his God. We've seen him saying prayers!"

The king was sad. But he had to keep the law.

Daniel was thrown to the lions.

The king fretted all through the night. "My best servant is probably being eaten right now," he sighed.

In the morning he went to the den.

"I'm still here," called Daniel. "God sent an angel to save me from the lions."

"That's wonderful news!" cried the king.

He had Daniel set free. "From now on, everyone in the world needs to know that Daniel's God is the best," he said.

37

Baby Jesus

The shepherds on the hillside could hardly believe their eyes.

"How can it be so bright, when it is night?" asked the youngest one sleepily.

"Look!" said the others. "And listen to the angels."

"Tonight is Good News night," declared the brightest angel. "A baby has been born in Bethlehem. He is God's Son. He has come to show everyone how they can be friends with God.

"Go and find him. He is cradled in a manger." The shepherds set off for the little town nearby.

"Why would anyone put their baby in a manger?" asked the youngest shepherd sleepily.

"I don't know," answered another. "Unless the inn was full and they had to sleep in the stable."

"Oh! Now we know where to look," said the third shepherd.

They went and they found little baby Jesus.

The shepherds told Jesus' mother Mary about the angels. She smiled. She already knew that her son was God's Son, come to bring joy to the world.

41

Jesus and His Disciples

Jesus grew up in Nazareth and learned to be a carpenter.

He knew inside that God had work for him to do. One day he set off, and began telling people how to live as God's friends.

Down by Lake Galilee he met some fishermen: Simon and his brother Andrew, James and his brother John.

"Come with me," said Jesus. "I want you to be my disciples and help me tell people about God."

The fishermen left their nets and followed him.

42

43

Now Jesus could go by boat to the towns around Lake Galilee.

At the end of one busy day, Jesus and his friends climbed aboard together.

Jesus fell asleep. While he was sleeping, a great storm blew up.

"Help us!" cried the disciples. "The boat is sinking."

Jesus stood up. He spoke to the wind and waves. "Shh. Lie down. Be quiet."

At once the storm stopped.

When Jesus wasn't listening, the disciples whispered to each other. "Who can Jesus be, to work a miracle like that?"

Jesus and the Little Girl

The father stood by the lake shore. He looked very upset. Then came a shout from the crowd:

"Here comes the boat! Jesus will be here very soon!"

The moment the boat was ashore, the father rushed to talk to Jesus.

"Please, please, please come and help. My little girl is very sick."

"Of course I'll come," replied Jesus.

The trouble was that all kinds of people wanted to see Jesus and to talk to him.

Before they reached the house, a messenger brought bad news.

"Your little girl has died."

"Don't worry," said Jesus to the father. Then to the people weeping outside the house he said, "No need for tears."

He went into the room were the girl lay on her bed.
He gently clasped her limp, cold hand.

"Little girl, get up now," he said.

The father and the mother could hardly believe
what they saw.

Their beautiful daughter opened her eyes and sat up.

Who could Jesus be, to work a miracle like that?

Jesus and the Children

Wherever Jesus went, people crowded around.

They wanted to learn how to live as God's friend.

They hoped to see a miracle.

The disciples tried to keep things organized.

When some mothers came with their children, they shook their heads.

"Jesus is too busy with important things," they said. "No children, please."

Jesus heard what they said. "Let the children come to me," he called. "They are special to God too."

He told a story.

51

A shepherd had a hundred sheep. One sheep – just one little sheep – went missing.

The shepherd made sure the ninety-nine were safe. Then he went looking for the one that was lost.

He kept looking until he found it. Then he carried it home.

"I'm so happy," he called to his friends.

"God is like that shepherd," said Jesus. "When anyone comes home to God, all the angels sing."

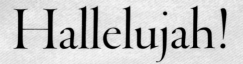

Hallelujah!

It was time for a festival in the city of Jerusalem.
Crowds were all going along the road there.
    Jesus came by, riding on a donkey.
    "Hallelujah!" they shouted. "We know
who Jesus is; he is God's royal king."
    They waved palm branches
like flags.

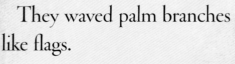

Not everyone liked Jesus.

"Who does Jesus think he is!" they muttered.

"We don't like his teaching.

"We don't believe the miracle stories.

"And now he's letting people think he's God's royal king.

"We'll put a stop to all this wickedness!"

They told lies about Jesus.

It was a Friday when they had him put to death on a cross.

With his last breath, Jesus said a prayer to God.

"Father God, forgive them. They don't know what they are doing."

Friends came and took Jesus' body. They laid it in a tomb.

Very early on the Sunday morning, some women came to say a last goodbye.

The tomb was empty.

Angels told them amazing news.

"Jesus is not here. God is stronger than death, and Jesus is alive again."

Soon after, the friends saw Jesus.

"I have done what I came to do," he told them.

"I have shown you how to be God's friends.
"I have opened the way to heaven, where those
who follow me will be safe in God's love for ever."

Jesus, friend of little children,
Be a friend to me;
Take my hand, and ever keep me
Close to thee.

A children's hymn